D1538706

LEARN

Japanese
WORDS

airplane
ひこうき
(hikooki)

office building
かいしゃビル
(kaisha biru)

library
としょかん
(toshokan)

LIBRARY

2100 OFFICE BUILDING

CITY BUS

bus
バス
(basu)

street
どうろ
(dooro)

BY M. J. YORK • ILLUSTRATED BY KATHLEEN PETELINSEK

Published by The Child's World®
1980 Lookout Drive • Mankato, MN 56003-1705
800-599-READ • www.childsworld.com

Acknowledgments
The Child's World®: Mary Berendes, Publishing Director
Translator: Kazue Kurahara
The Design Lab: Design
Red Line Editorial: Editorial direction
Amnet: Production

Copyright © 2015 by The Child's World®
All rights reserved. No part of this book may be reproduced or
utilized in any form or by any means without written permission
from the publisher.

ISBN 9781626873766
LCCN 2014930647

Printed in the United States of America
Mankato, MN
July, 2015
PA02273

ABOUT THE AUTHOR

M. J. York is a children's author and
editor living in Minnesota. She loves
learning about different people
and places.

ABOUT THE ILLUSTRATOR

Kathleen Petelinsek loves to draw
and paint. She also loves to travel
to exotic countries where people
speak foreign languages. She lives
in Minnesota with her husband, two
daughters, two dogs, a fluffy cat, and
three chickens.

CONTENTS

Introduction to Japanese

Japanese is the language of Japan and its islands. It is a major world language. At least 125 million people speak Japanese. Many forms of Japanese are spoken throughout the islands.

Japanese is related to the Korean language. It is also related to other Asian languages. Chinese writing has influenced the language. Many new words come from English and European languages, too. But Japanese has changed very little for centuries.

Written Japanese uses three systems of characters. Kanji uses Chinese symbols called characters. (No kanji is used in this book.) In Chinese, these characters stand for words or ideas. But in Japanese, the characters can stand for sounds or for Japanese words.

The other two systems are katakana and hiragana. Each uses symbols that were parts of Chinese characters. Each symbol stands for a sound. Hiragana looks more rounded. In this book, hiragana characters are shown in red. Katakana looks more angular. Katakana is used to write many words that are borrowed from other languages. In this book, katakana characters are shown in purple.

Writing Japanese sounds using the English alphabet is called romaji. It is pronounced like English with a few differences.

Most syllables in a word should take the same amount of time to say. Syllables with double vowels (aa, ee, ii, oo, or uu) are held twice as long.

The letter F is said like you are whistling it. Purse your lips to say it.

The letter R is trilled or rolled. It sounds close to a letter L.

My Home
わたしのいえ
(Watashi no ie)

window
まど
(mado)

lamp
ランプ
(ranpu)

bathroom
バスルーム
(basu ruumu)

bedroom
ベッドルーム
(beddo ruumu)

television
テレビ
(terebi)

kitchen
キッチン
(kicchin)

cat
ねこ
(neko)

living room
リビングルーム
(ribingu ruumu)

sofa
ソファー
(sofaa)

chair
いす
(isu)

table
テーブル
(teeburu)

In the Morning
あさのじかん
(Asa no jikan)

dresser
たんす
(tansu)

clock
とけい
(tokee)

teddy bear
テディーベアー
(tedii beaa)

doll
にんぎょう
(ningyoo)

pillow
まくら
(makura)

bed
ベッド
(beddo)

blanket
ブランケット
(buranketto)

At the Park
こうえんで
(Kooen de)

Let's play soccer!
サッカーをしよう!
(Sakkaa o shiyoo!)

sky
そら
(sora)

friend
ともだち
(tomodachi)

friend
ともだち
(tomodachi)

soccer ball
サッカーボール
(sakkaa booru)

bird
とり
(tori)

MORE USEFUL WORDS

game
しあい
shiai

sports
スポーツ
supootsu

sun
たいよう
(taiyoo)

swing
ブランコ
(buranko)

clouds
くも
(kumo)

playground
あそびば
(asobiba)

slide
すべりだい
(suberidai)

water
みず
(mizu)

pond
いけ
(ike)

flower
はな
(hana)

duck
あひる
(ahiru)

Around Town
まちで
(Machi de)

library
としょかん
(toshokan)

firefighter
しょうぼうし
(shoobooshi)

LIBRARY

Excuse me.
すみません。
(Sumimasen.)

woman
おんなのひと
(onna no hito)

man
おとこのひと
(otoko no hito)

police officer
おまわりさん
(omawarisan)

street
どうろ
(dooro)

14

airplane
ひこうき
(hikooki)

office building
かいしゃビル
(kaisha biru)

building
たてもの
(tatemono)

bus
バス
(basu)

2100
OFFICE
BUILDING

CITY BUS

MORE USEFUL WORDS

truck
トラック
(torakku)

train
でんしゃ
(densha)

stop
とまれ
(tomare)

go
すすめ
(susume)

My Birthday Party
わたしのたんじょうびパーティー
(Watashi no tanjoobi paatii)

grandmother
おばあさん
(obaasan)

grandfather
おじいさん
(ojiisan)

I turned six.
ろくさいになったよ。
(Rokusai ni nattayo.)

MORE USEFUL WORDS

one いち *(ichi)*	eleven じゅういち *(juuichi)*
two に *(ni)*	twelve じゅうに *(juuni)*
three さん *(san)*	thirteen じゅうさん *(juusan)*
four し *(shi)*	fourteen じゅうし *(juushi)*
five ご *(go)*	fifteen じゅうご *(juugo)*
six ろく *(roku)*	sixteen じゅうろく *(juuroku)*
seven しち *(shichi)*	seventeen じゅうしち *(juushichi)*
eight はち *(hachi)*	eighteen じゅうはち *(juuhachi)*
nine きゅう *(kyuu)*	nineteen じゅうきゅう *(juukyuu)*
ten じゅう *(juu)*	twenty にじゅう *(nijuu)*

older brother
おにいさん
(oniisan)

younger sister
いもうと
(imooto)

cake
ケーキ
(keeki)

older sister
おねえさん
(oneesan)

younger brother
おとうと
(otooto)

Preparing Dinner
ばんごはんのじゅんび
(Bangohan no junbi)

bread
パン
(pan)

electric stove
でんきレンジ
(denki renji)

pot
なべ
(nabe)

I am hungry.
おなかがすいたね。
(Onaka ga suitane.)

glass
グラス
(gurasu)

rice
ごはん
(gohan)

plate
さら
(sara)

meat
にく
(niku)

fork
フォーク
(fooku)

knife
ナイフ
(naifu)

spoon
スプーン
(supuun)

Night Time
よるのじかん
(Yoru no jikan)

Good night!
おやすみなさい。
(Oyasuminasai.)

MORE USEFUL WORDS

Today is Friday!
きょうはきんようびです。
(Kyoo wa kin-yoobi desu.)

Yesterday was Thursday.
きのうはもくようびでした。
(Kinoo wa mokuyoobi deshita.)

Tomorrow is Saturday.
あしたはどようびです。
(Ashita wa doyoobi desu.)

shower
シャワー
(shawaa)

bathtub
バスタブ
(basutabu)

I'm sleepy!
ねむい。
(Nemui.)

MORE USEFUL WORDS

ten
じゅう
(juu)

twenty
にじゅう
(nijuu)

thirty
さんじゅう
(sanjuu)

forty
よんじゅう
(yonjuu)

fifty
ごじゅう
(gojuu)

sixty
ろくじゅう
(rokujuu)

seventy
ななじゅう
(nanajuu)

eighty
はちじゅう
(hachijuu)

ninety
きゅうじゅう
(kyuujuu)

one hundred
ひゃく
(hyaku)

Yes (polite)
はい
(hai)

Yes (casual)
うん
(un)

No (polite)
いいえ
(iie)

No (casual)
ううん
(uun)

winter
ふゆ
(fuyu)

spring
はる
(haru)

summer
なつ
(natsu)

fall
あき
(aki)

good-bye!
さようなら。
(Sayoonara.)

January
いちがつ
(ichigatsu)

February
にがつ
(nigatsu)

March
さんがつ
(sangatsu)

April
しがつ
(shigatsu)

May
ごがつ
(gogatsu)

June
ろくがつ
(rokugatsu)

July
しちがつ
(shichigatsu)

August
はちがつ
(hachigatsu)

September
くがつ
(kugatsu)

October
じゅうがつ
(juugatsu)

November
じゅういち
がつ
(juuichigatsu)

December
じゅうにがつ
(juunigatsu)